Keats and his Circle

Keats and his Circle

AN ALBUM OF PORTRAITS
COLLECTED AND PRESENTED
BY

JOANNA RICHARDSON

CASSELL

LONDON

Cassell Ltd.
35 Red Lion Square, London WC1R 4SG
and at Sydney, Auckland, Toronto, Johannesburg,
an affiliate of
Macmillan Publishing Co., Inc.,
New York.

First published 1980

ISBN 0 304 30711 4

Set, printed and bound in Great Britain by
Fakenham Press Limited, Fakenham, Norfolk

CONTENTS

INTRODUCTION

Some months ago, I was spending a few days with the great-granddaughter of Fanny Brawne. She showed me a collection of family photographs. There was one of Fanny's husband, Louis Lindon, and there were several of their children. There were two *carte-de-visite* photographs of Fanny's sister, Margaret, and one of Margaret's husband, the Chevalier da Cunha, sometime Brazilian Minister to Vienna. It was an enthralling collection, and it was still unknown—but to me the centrepiece was missing. Mrs. Goodsell brought out a final box. Inside I found a small, embossed red leather case which was fastened with a gilt clasp. One half was lined with magenta velvet, imprinted with a pattern of fuchsias. The other half held an ambrotype, brilliantly clear, in a gilt frame engraved with arabesques. It was the living likeness of Fanny Brawne.

Until now we had had to imagine her from a miniature and a silhouette. We had had to guess her appearance from the Titian figure which Severn thought so strongly resembled her. Now, for the first time, we could see her.

She was exactly as Keats had described her: 'beautiful and elegant, graceful, ... fashionable and strange'. Strange, indeed: she was almost an exotic, Spanish figure. 'Shall I give you Miss Brawn[e]?' Keats asked his brother. 'She is about my height—with a fine style of countenance of the lengthen'd sort—she wants sentiment in every feature—she manages to make her hair look well—her nostrills are fine—though a little painful—he[r] mouth is bad and good—he[r] Profil is better than her full-face which indeed is not full but pale and thin without showing any bone.' There was no lack of sentiment in this portrait. There was extraordinary dignity. There were serenity and style; there was also an unmistakable sadness. This ambrotype confirmed not only Keats's description, but Fanny Brawne's—Fanny Lindon's—depth of character. As one already knew from her letters to Keats's sister, she was a woman of sense and sensibility. She was wonderfully undisappointing.

With this ambrotype there were three others, taken of her children: Edmund, Herbert and Margaret. As if this were not enough, Dr. Fernando Paradinas gave me three unpublished photographs of his great-great-grandparents, Fanny Keats and her husband Valentin Llanos. He also gave me photographs of the portraits which had been painted of them in their old age.

This collection, it seemed to me, deserved a book to itself. It was the moment to produce an album of pictures of Keats and his circle.

Here, then, assembled from private and public collections, from books and galleries and family archives, is a visual impression of Keats, his family and

1

friends. Haydon has done a life-mask of Keats—most haunting of all likenesses of him. Severn has drawn the living and the dying Keats, and recalled him, again and again, after death. Charles Brown, too, has drawn his dearest friend; Woodhouse has commissioned the Girometti medallion ('quite a piece of magic,' considered Brown). Since I have had to be selective, I have chosen only the more distinguished likenesses of Keats that were made in his brief lifetime, and the more authentic ones made after his death. The MacDowell bust, for example, was said to have been sculpted under the supervision of Fanny Keats and Fanny Brawne, and Severn's recollections of Keats at Wentworth Place and on Hampstead Heath deserve a place which no one could accord to the Whitney bust of Keats in Hampstead Parish Church.

More than once the Keats circle portray one another. Severn paints Carlino Brown and John Hamilton Reynolds; Haydon paints Dr. Darling. William Hilton records John Taylor, and Marianne Hunt cuts her husband's silhouette. Sometimes the portraits are familiar, sometimes they are little known; a number of them are published here for the first time. After I set to work on this book, Dr. Paradinas found two further likenesses of Fanny Keats. One of these he discovered, unframed, among some family papers. It was an earlier portrait than any which we had seen. Mr. R. P. Cockerton generously added a watercolour of James Taylor, senior, and a daguerreotype of John Taylor: the first known actual likeness of Keats's publisher.

This album does not claim to be an exhaustive record, but I have included everything of interest which is in the Goodsell archives, for we cannot know enough about Fanny Brawne; and her descendants have played a sometimes significant part in the development of Keats's fame. I have of course included all the new pictures from the Paradinas collection, but I have not reproduced all the portraits of Fanny Keats in her old age, for there is little difference between them. I have, however, published some photographs of her children, who presented their uncle's letters to the English nation; they were the second generation of the Keats family. Brown's son is here, for he was born in Keats's lifetime, and Keats was perhaps aware of his existence; Carlino was to be aware of his father's friendship, and in later years he sent Keatsiana to Sir Charles Dilke. Sir Charles, alas, has earned his place as much as his father, Sir Wentworth, whom the poet knew as 'Dilke's Boy'. Whatever the munificence of the Dilke bequest to Hampstead, Sir Charles burned a mass of Keats papers, including some letters in Keats's hand. Three other latter-day figures deserve recording as honorary members of Keats's circle. Richard Monckton Milnes, the first Lord Houghton, introduced Keats to the English public in 1848. Harry Buxton Forman published the love letters thirty years later, and his monumental editions of the correspondence will never be entirely superseded. Sir Sidney Colvin, in his turn, edited Keats's letters, and—in 1887—published the best of the early biographies.

I have, I hope, included in this album all the relations, friends and critics mentioned in Keats's letters: at least all those whose likenesses have been sculpted, painted, drawn, photographed, or cut out of paper. I have also

2

included—where I could—portraits of people whom the poet knew but did not name: John Clarke, his headmaster at Enfield; George Reynolds of Little Britain; Dr. Darling and Dr. Lambe, who attended him before he went to Italy; William Ewing, who knew him in Rome. I have included certain people whom he did not meet—but who figure none the less in his letters: Edmund Kean, whom he admired on stage; Gifford, who published a savage review of *Endymion* in the *Quarterly*; Lockhart, who attacked him in *Blackwood's Edinburgh Magazine*; Byron, who mistakenly thought him snuffed out by an article. I have gone further afield, and included Charles Brown's parents, and Severn's family, and Jane Reynolds's husband, Thomas Hood. I have also introduced Mrs. J. H. Reynolds, whose courting was reflected in Keats's letters (it was for her that Reynolds went 'into Devonshire').

I am very much aware of those who figured in the life of Keats and were not, it seems, recorded on canvas. There is no known portrait of Mr. Abbey, or of Mrs. Brawne; there is no acknowledged picture of the poet's 'oak friend', William Haslam. Thomas Richards and William Mayor were among Keats's correspondents, but we have yet to meet them face to face. The Davenports remain elusive, so do the Jefferys of Teignmouth, the Gisbornes, the Olliers and the Snooks. Joseph Ritchie, who met Keats at the Immortal Dinner, earned fame as an explorer, but there appears to be no portrait of him. Mancur remains a mystery; so, alas, does Isabella Jones. 'Walk to Somerset House,' she told Taylor in 1819, 'and give me your candid opinion upon my likeness by Chalon, no. 895.' I have not yet detected no. 895, nor have I found any picture of Jane Cox, the Reynolds's cousin, and Keats's Charmian. There are, I believe, some photographs of James Augustus Hessey and other familiar members of the Keats circle, but they have not yet made their appearance. I hope that this album will cause some forgotten portraits to be discovered.

I owe my largest debt to Mrs. N. F. Goodsell, the great-granddaughter of Fanny Brawne, for her generous hospitality and for allowing me to use the historic pictures in her possession; this album owes its existence to her kindness and enthusiasm. I am extremely grateful to Dr. Ernesto Paradinas, who has let me reproduce the unpublished pictures of Fanny Keats and her husband, and to Dr. Fernando Paradinas, great-great-nephew of Keats, for his hospitality and for his constant interest and help. I must express my gratitude to Miss Ella Keats Whiting for letting me use the silhouettes of George and Georgiana Keats. I am much indebted to Lady Birkenhead and to Mr. Guy Severn who have very kindly let me use the self-portrait of Joseph Severn and the watercolour of his wife. I gladly thank Sir John Dilke for permission to reproduce the pictures in his possession, and Mr. Christopher Dilke and Captain S. W. Roskill for answering my enquiries. I am also most grateful to Mr. Ken Guichard for letting me use the watercolour miniature of William Dilke. The late Mrs. Osborne, granddaughter of Charles Brown, sent me a photograph of a sketch of Carlino by Seymour Kirkup. La Contessa Gigliucci has kindly allowed me to reproduce the Novello family picture and the silhouettes of Mr. and Mrs. John Clarke. Mr. R. P. Cockerton has generously let me use the watercolour of James Taylor, senior, and the fine daguerreotype of his great-great-uncle, John Taylor. Mr. D. Carr Taylor has allowed me to reproduce his portrait of John Taylor, and Mr. T. J. Cartwright-Taylor has let me use the drawing of John Taylor in his possession. Mrs G. D. Hessell has given me her consent to reproduce the portrait of Mrs George Reynolds; Mr. T. P. F. Miller has kindly let me use Haydon's portrait of Dr. Darling, and the Reverend W. B. Scott has given me permission to reproduce the silhouette of T. J. Hogg. I am of course most grateful to the Director of Libraries and Arts of the London Borough of Camden for permission to use material at Keats House, Hampstead; and I gladly express my thanks to Mrs. Gee, Miss van Reenen and Mrs. Archer for their unremitting help at Keats House. I much appreciate the assistance I have had from Mr. Charles Boydell of Cassell Ltd.

Hampstead,   JOANNA RICHARDSON
February 1980.

Benjamin Bailey was born in Cambridgeshire on 5 June 1791. In the autumn of 1816 he matriculated at Oxford; he intended to enter the church. In the spring and summer of 1817 he met Keats in London, saw much of him, and invited him to Oxford. Keats spent most of September at Magdalen Hall, where he wrote the third book of *Endymion*, and 'had regularly a Boat on the Isis, and explored all the streams about'. He and Bailey lost themselves in literary discussions, and parted with mutual admiration and affection.

Their friendship was shortlived, for Keats was angered by Bailey's 'very bad conduct' to Marianne Reynolds, and by his hasty marriage to Hamilton Gleig, the daughter of the Bishop of Brechin. Their correspondence ended, though thirty years later Bailey told Monckton Milnes that Keats was 'the most *loveable* creature' he had known. In 1831 Bailey emigrated to Ceylon as senior colonial chaplain; in time he became Archdeacon of Colombo. He died in London on 25 June 1853.

Two miniatures and a silhouette show him in his youth.

Left: 'Yesterday I dined with Hazlitt, Barnes, and Wilkie at Haydon's. The topic was the Duke of Wellington very amusingly pro and con'd.' So Keats told Benjamin Bailey on 25 May 1818. It was the only mention of Barnes in Keats's correspondence, but it was probably not their only meeting. Thomas Barnes (1785–1841) was editor of *The Times* from 1817 until his death. He had been associated with Leigh Hunt and Hazlitt as a writer for the *Examiner*. This portrait of him was painted by Sir William Newton.

Right: 'On Sunday I . . . dined with Haydon, met Hazlitt and Bewick there,' Keats reported to his brothers in mid-January 1818. William Bewick, the Darlington artist, was much impressed by these 'very intellectual dinners', and wrote home that he had met 'Keats the poet, Hazlitt the critic. . . .' Bewick (1796–1866) makes a few appearances in Keats's letters, and he records him, briefly, in his own correspondence. This engraving of Bewick was done by J. Brown after a painting by L. Macartan.

George Brummell, wrote his biographer, 'occasionally paid a visit to his aunt Brawn; and one of the earliest episodes remembered of his childhood is, that he was one day guilty of crying most bitterly, because he could not eat any more of her ample damson tart'. Aunt Brawn was Mrs. Samuel Brawne, grandmother of Fanny Brawne. These portraits show Miss Brummell, by Thomas Gainsborough, and the Brummell children, by Sir Joshua Reynolds. George Brummell, whose sash is here undone by his elder brother, was to be renowned as Beau Brummell. Fanny Brawne was to be remarkable for her elegance.

9

Fanny Brawne was born on her parents' farm in the hamlet of West End, Hampstead, on 9 August 1800. In the summer of 1818 her mother—then a widow—rented Charles Brown's half of Wentworth Place, and became friendly with the Dilkes next door. It was at the Dilkes', that autumn, that Keats met Fanny Brawne; within the week he 'wrote himself her vassal'. At Christmas they were privately engaged; in April 1819, when the Dilkes left Hampstead, the Brawnes moved into Wentworth Place, and Keats entered the most fertile weeks of his poetic life. Fanny loved Keats with devotion. After his death, she wore mourning for seven years. Not until 1833—twelve years after Keats had died—did she finally marry Louis Lindo. They spent much of their married life on the Continent, in an attempt to improve Fanny's health, but when they returned to London in 1859 she was a confirmed invalid. She died on 4 December 1865, and she is buried in Brompton Cemetery. 'She was rather taller than Keats,' wrote Severn, '& strongly resembling the splendid figure (in a white dress) in Titians picture of sacred & profane love.' Severn often used to visit the Borghese Gallery in Rome to admire this accidental likeness. (*Opposite.*)

Above left: Fanny Brawne, aged twenty-eight. This silhouette was cut by Augustin Édouart between January and June 1829.

Above right: Fanny Brawne. This miniature, by an unknown artist, was painted at about the time of her marriage to Louis Lindo, on 15 June 1833.

11

Fanny Brawne, Mrs. Louis Lindon. From an ambrotype, probably English, taken in the early 1850s.

Louis Lindo—later Lindon (1812–72). This studio photograph, taken in later life, is the only known likeness of Fanny Brawne's husband.

13

14

Above: Edmund Vernon Lindon, the elder son of Fanny Brawne, was born on 26 July 1834. Traveller and journalist, he died in India on 25 August 1877. The first of these *carte-de-visite* photographs (*left*) was taken by Gustave Le Gray in Paris at about the time of Edmund's thirtieth birthday. The second photograph, by C. L. Cramer, was taken in San Francisco some time later, and shows him wearing the Cossack dress which he had acquired on his travels.

Opposite: Fanny Brawne's children. Edmund, Herbert and Margaret Lindon, from ambrotypes taken in the 1850s.

15

Herbert Valentin Lindon, the younger son of Fanny Brawne, and the godson of Valentin Llanos, was born in Bayonne on 22 May 1838. Educated in Germany, he became a civil servant on the family's return to England. He later retired from the Civil Service, and joined the Imperial Continental Gas Association, as chief inspector of Continental accounts. That year—1880—he married Euphemia, daughter of Admiral George Hathorn, and for some years they lived largely in Vienna. After the death of Margaret da Cunha, the last of the Brawne family, Herbert changed his name to Brawne-Lindon. In 1899 he resigned his Vienna post, and the family settled in Folkestone. Here he died on 6 October 1909.

Colvin, in his life of Keats, wrote that Fanny Brawne belonged to the 'English hawk blonde type, with aquiline nose and retreating forehead'; a colleague of Herbert Brawne-Lindon's recalled his 'very hawk-like countenance'. This photograph of him comes from a family photograph album. It was taken—by J. Lowy of Vienna—in early middle age.

Top: Figures in a landscape: Herbert Brawne-Lindon (*centre*) with his sister Margaret (*left*), his wife and a friend. This photograph was taken in Austria at the end of the last century.

Bottom: Herbert Brawne-Lindon, at the age of about sixty-seven. A studio photograph by C. Pietzner, Vienna.

17

Top: Herbert Brawne-Lindon in his later years. From a photograph by E. Drory of Vienna.

Bottom: Two grandchildren of Fanny Brawne. Frances and Louis, daughter and son of Herbert Brawne-Lindon. This studio photograph dates from about 1886.

Top: Herbert and Louis Brawne-Lindon. This distinctly Forsyte photograph of father and son was taken in about 1890.

Bottom: Margaret Emily Walworth Lindon, the only daughter of Fanny
Brawne, was born on 10 August 1844: the day after her mother's forty-fourth
birthday. She remained unmarried. Relatives recalled her, in her later years:
a white-haired figure in a bath-chair at Folkestone. She died in Lausanne on
1 June 1907. This *carte-de-visite* photograph of her as a young woman was
taken by Alexander J. Grossmann, of Dover.

Opposite: 'Tell Tootts I wish I could pitch her a basket of grapes,' wrote Keats to Mrs. Brawne from Naples, on 24 October 1820. Tootts was the nickname of Margaret Brawne, Fanny's younger sister, to whom he had given an amethyst brooch and sent his love and remembrance in his letters. Margaret, born on 10 April 1809, was renowned for her beauty. In 1833 she married a Brazilian diplomat, João Pereira da Cunha, sometime Minister to Vienna. They had no children of their own, but Margaret was much loved by Fanny's sons and daughters. She outlived her husband and died in Lausanne on 14 June 1887. This *carte-de-visite* photograph of her was taken by Steinberger & Bauer, of Frankfurt.

Above: João Antonio Pereira, Chevalier da Cunha, was born near Lisbon on 12 October 1802. He was Comptroller to the Empress Doña Leopoldina of Brazil before he was appointed to the Brazilian Ministry of Foreign Affairs. In 1826 he was transferred to the Brazilian Legation in London, where he was briefly chargé d'affaires; in 1827 he was chargé d'affaires in Paris. The following year he was transferred to Berlin, where he stayed until the Mission was closed in 1830. On 30 November 1833 he married Margaret Brawne, and in 1836 he was appointed Resident Minister to Vienna. Here he remained with his wife until his retirement in 1841. He had died by November 1883. This photograph of him was taken by Bertall, in Paris. The *carte-de-visite* photograph of his wife, inscribed 'dear Aunt Margaret da Cunha', was taken by Heer-Tschudi & Welti, of Lausanne.

21

22

Opposite top: Samuel Brawne, brother of Fanny, was born on 26 July 1804, and he was a schoolboy when Keats knew him. He became a youth with a sense of style ('he has got a white coat,' his sister reported, when he was seventeen, 'and I am afraid fancies himself a man'). He took a clerical job in an office, and, by a strange coincidence, James Armitage Brown, the nephew of Charles Brown, 'was at the same office with Brawne and sat at the same desk with him'. Samuel Brawne died of tuberculosis on 28 March 1828. This miniature of him was painted by an unknown artist.

Opposite bottom: The parents of Charles Armitage Brown. William Brown, from the portrait painted in May 1801; and Jane Brown (later Mrs. Joseph Rennoit Browne).

Above: Henry Brown, one of the brothers of Charles Armitage Brown. Henry, wrote his great-niece, Mrs. Osborne, 'was an officer on a ship and caught fever and died in the West Indies, he was under 20 years of age. . . . He was a midshipman, his ship after leaving the West Indies returned to Europe and took part in the Battle of Trafalgar. Henry was a pretty youth according to his portrait.'

24

Charles Armitage Brown was born in Lambeth on 14 April 1787: the sixth son of William Brown, a Scottish broker, and his Welsh wife. At school he met Charles Wentworth Dilke, and established a friendship which was to last for some thirty years. At fourteen, Brown left school for a counting-house and a salary of £40 a year; by the time he was eighteen he had gone to join his brother John's firm in St. Petersburg. The Russian episode brought commercial failure, but it inspired his comic opera *Narensky*, which was produced at Drury Lane in 1814. The following year the builders started work on a modest house in Hampstead which Brown and Dilke were to share; and Dilke, adopting his family name, called it Wentworth Place.

It was in the late summer of 1817, on the Hampstead Road, that Brown first met Keats, and 'inwardly desired his acquaintanceship, if not his friendship'. Keats was twenty-one; he was drawn to the wise and genial man of thirty. They were soon 'very thick'; and, in the summer of 1818, they left together on a walking tour of the Lake District and Highlands. On 1 December, Tom Keats died of tuberculosis, and Brown invited Keats to live with him. He charged £5 a month for board, but it was never merely a business arrangement. Brown was devoted to Keats, and Keats had assured himself of the daily companionship he needed. Brown not only encouraged Keats, but copied out his poetry. In the summer of 1819 they worked together on a drama, *Otho the Great*. Brown was 'head Nurse' when Keats fell ill, early in 1820; he was unaware of the gravity of his condition when, that summer, he himself left for another Scottish holiday. By the time he returned, Joseph Severn had sailed with Keats for Italy. After the poet's death, Brown moved to Italy himself; there he met Byron, lived for a while with Severn, and became a friend of Walter Savage Landor. It was at Landor's, at Fiesole, that he met Richard Monckton Milnes. Brown had watched, with vigilance, over Keats's fame; he had written a life of Keats, but no publisher would take it. He settled for a while in Devon; and on 29 December 1836, at the Plymouth Athenaeum, he gave the first public lecture on his friend. He printed his unpublished poems—among them the Bright Star Sonnet—in *The Plymouth and Devonport Weekly Journal*. He showed portraits of him at a local exhibition. In 1841, on the eve of his emigration to New Zealand, he asked Monckton Milnes to publish the life and poems of Keats, and sent him all the papers in his possession. Brown died in New Zealand on 5 June 1842; on his tomb, under the shadow of Mount Taranaki, is the inscription: 'Friend of Keats'.

This bust, the only known likeness of Keats's 'capital friend', was done by Andrew Wilson in Florence in 1828.

Charles (Carlino) Brown was born in 1820; his birth certificate records him as 'the son of Charles Brown and Abigail Brown (born Donaghue)'. Abigail had been Brown's housekeeper at Wentworth Place; he had chosen her, so Carlino said later, with cynical detachment, 'for her splendid physique, for the sake of the offspring'. Yet though he hardly admired her, Brown respected her enough to marry her, as she insisted, in a Catholic church; and though a Catholic marriage was not then valid in England, he always considered himself to be her husband.

In 1822, Brown took Carlino with him to Italy. Two miniatures by Joseph Severn show the boy at the ages of three and six. The drawing of him, by Seymour Kirkup, was made when he was nine.

26

As a young man, Carlino showed a talent for engineering; but, when he returned to England with his father, his prospects in England and Europe were uncertain, and Brown decided, for his sake, to emigrate to New Zealand. They sailed in 1841; Brown died in 1842, and left his son to make his career alone. Carlino became a member of the House of Representatives, and Civil Commissioner at Taranaki. He was Commandant of the Militia and Volunteers in the Maori campaigns of 1860 and 1863. He was run over and killed by a train in September 1901.

This photograph of Carlino—then Major Charles Brown—was taken at the end of his life.

'You speak of Lord Byron and me,' wrote Keats to George and Georgiana Keats, in September 1819. 'There is this great difference between us. He describes what he sees—I describe what I imagine. Mine is the hardest task.' George Gordon, 6th Lord Byron (1788–1824): a sketch by Count d'Orsay, made in May 1823.

In August 1820, just before he left for Italy, Keats told Charles Brown: 'I am
to be introduced, before I set out, to a Dr Clarke, a physician settled at Rome,
who promises to befriend me in every way.' Clark found him rooms at 26,
Piazza di Spagna, opposite his own lodgings; and Severn reported that there
were 'no bounds' to his attention. He 'went all over Rome for a certain kind of
fish, and got it,' and his wife prepared it for Keats; he came over '4 & 5 times
a day'. He soon recognised, however, that the prospect was hopeless. He was
among those who attended Keats's funeral. He later became physician to the
King of the Belgians, the Duchess of Kent, and Queen Victoria. He was
created a baronet in 1837. The watercolour portrait (*left*) of Sir James Clark,
M.D. (1788–1870) was painted by Hope James Stewart in 1849; it is owned
by the National Galleries of Scotland. The formal portrait, in oils, was
probably painted by John Andrews; it comes from the Royal College of
Physicians. The daguerreotype (*overleaf*) is owned by the Royal College of
Surgeons.

29

30

Charles Cowden Clarke, the son of the headmaster at Enfield, was a notable early influence on Keats. Eight years his senior—he was born in 1787—he introduced him to Spenser, and to Chapman's Homer: an introduction which, he said, inspired 'the finest of all his Sonnetts'. He also presented him to Leigh Hunt. Lecturer and man of letters, Cowden Clarke helped Monckton Milnes with his biography, and never lost his admiration for Keats. He married Mary, the daughter of Vincent Novello. They appear together, in their younger days, in the Novello family picture. This portrait of Cowden Clarke was painted by an unknown artist in about 1834. He died in 1877, and his wife died in 1898.

31

John Clarke was born in 1757. He was an assistant in a solicitor's office at Northampton before he entered the teaching profession. In 1786 he set up a school at Enfield, in Middlesex, and the following year he married Ann Isabella Stott, the stepdaughter of his previous employer. Among his pupils at Enfield were the brothers of Mrs. Keats, and she in turn sent her three sons to the school. Keats owed much to the liberal education he received from Clarke. After his retirement, Clarke moved to Ramsgate with his wife, their son Charles, and an unmarried daughter. He died in December 1820.

'Last Sunday I took a walk towards highgate and in the lane that winds by
the side of Lord Mansfield's park I met Mr Green our Demonstrator at Guy's
in conversation with Coleridge ... I walked with him [Coleridge] a[t] his
alderman-after-dinner pace for near two miles I suppose. In those two Miles
he broached a thousand things ... He was civil enough to ask me to call on
him at Highgate ...' Keats described the meeting to his brother George on 15
April 1819. This portrait of Samuel Taylor Coleridge (1772–1834) was
painted by W. Allston in 1814.

Above: Sir Sidney Colvin (1845–1927). Sometime Slade Professor of Fine Art at Cambridge, he was also Keeper of Prints and Drawings at the British Museum. His literary work included a notable life of Keats; it appeared in 1887, the same year as his edition of Keats's letters. This photograph of Colvin was taken in 1921.

Opposite top: Sir Astley Cooper (1768–1841). The famous surgeon was the senior anatomy lecturer at Guy's Hospital when Keats registered there as a medical student in October 1815. Keats attended his lectures. This portrait of Sir Astley Cooper, by Sir Thomas Lawrence, hangs in the Council Room of the Royal College of Surgeons.

Opposite bottom: On 28 February 1820, Keats wrote to John Hamilton Reynolds: 'Mr B.C. has sent me not only his Sicilian Story but yesterday his Dramatic Scenes—this is very polite and I shall do what I can to make him sensible I think so. I confess they tease me—they are composed of Amiability—the Seasons, the Leaves, the Moon &c. upon which he rings (according to Hunt's expression) triple bob majors.' 'Mr B.C.' was Bryan Waller Procter, better known as Barry Cornwall (1787–1874). This engraving of him by W. Brockedon is dated 2 November 1830.

35

Above: The Quarterly Review for April 1818 published what professed to be a criticism of *Endymion*. It was in fact a savage personal attack on Keats, whom Leigh Hunt had acclaimed as a poet of the future. There had long been a feud between Hunt and the editor of the *Quarterly*. 'My own domestic criticism,' wrote Keats, 'has given me pain beyond comparison beyond what Blackwood or the Quarterly could possibly inflict.' He was not 'snuffed out' by the article, which roused public protest in the *Morning Chronicle*, and led Richard Woodhouse to exclaim: 'God help the Critic, whoever he be!' The anonymous critic was John Wilson Croker (1780–1857), secretary to the Admiralty, politician and man of letters. Macaulay 'detested him more than cold boiled veal'. This portrait of Croker was painted by W. Owen.

Opposite: 'I hope you have Darling's advice, on whose skill I have the greatest reliance.' So Haydon wrote to Keats in July 1820. Darling had first examined Keats on 22 June; he later called in Dr. William Lambe, and, on their joint advice, Keats went to Italy. Darling was Haydon's doctor; he was also the doctor of John Taylor, who had presumably recommended him to Keats. Munk's *Roll of the Royal College of Physicians* records:

'George Darling, M.D., was born in Edinburgh and educated as a surgeon, in which capacity he entered the service of the East India company and took two or three voyages to India. He settled in London as a general practitioner in partnership with Mr. (afterwards Dr.) Neil Arnott. Relinquishing that department of practice he graduated doctor of medicine at Aberdeen 1st April, 1815; and was admitted a Licentiate of the College of Physicians 22nd December, 1819. He settled in Russell-square and enjoyed for many years a lucrative practice in the northern districts of the metropolis. He was much employed by artists, and numbered among his friends and patients Hilton, Haydon, Wilkie, Chantrey, and Sir Thomas Lawrence. He was also intimate with Sir James Mackintosh, whose family gave Dr. Darling, as a token of friendship for his assiduous medical attendance on their father, a valuable diamond snuff-box which Sir James had received as a present from the queen of Portugal. Dr. Darling died at Russell-square 30th April, 1862.'

This portrait of Dr. Darling was painted by Benjamin Robert Haydon.

Peter de Wint, the son of a Dutch–American physician, was born at Stone, in Staffordshire, on 21 January 1784. At the age of eighteen he went to London as apprentice to a painter and engraver, in whose house he met the young William Hilton. Their friendship was 'one of the longest and truest in the history of art', and it was strengthened by De Wint's marriage to Hilton's sister. De Wint became a fashionable painter in watercolours. Keats apparently met him through Taylor or Hessey, and knew him better than readers of the letters might suppose. De Wint was one of the five friends who each contributed £10 towards his expenses in Italy. De Wint died on 30 June 1849. The *Athenaeum* declared: 'He has taken his place in Water-Colour Art, and will be missed and remembered, with Girtin and Turner,—for the impulse which they gave to a style of painting peculiarly English.' These miniatures of Peter and Harriet de Wint, by an unknown artist, are now in the Usher Gallery, Lincoln.

Charles Wentworth Dilke was born on 8 December 1789, the son of an Admiralty clerk who was working at Portsmouth with Dickens's father. He himself became a clerk at the Navy Pay Office, Somerset House. His marriage to Maria Walker brought him an only son, Charley, and 'a most complete happiness'. His 'most affectionate friendship', said his grandson, was with Keats; they were friends by September 1817, and 'capital friends' when the new year began. When Keats lived with Brown at Wentworth Place, they were briefly neighbours. Dilke, wrote Keats, 'was a Man who cannot feel he has a personal identity unless he has made up his Mind about every thing'. He found Dilke too opinionated, but he appreciated his good sense, sociability and literary tastes. After Keats's death, Dilke became financial adviser to Fanny Keats and the Brawnes; he looked after George Keats's English affairs. He quarrelled finally with Brown over George's alleged misdeeds, and he helped Monckton Milnes 'with letters and remembrances'. Editor of the *Athenaeum* and manager of the *Daily News*, he became a distinguished literary figure. He died on 10 August 1864.

This portrait, by an unknown artist, was painted in about 1825.

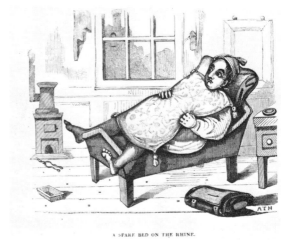

A SPARE BED ON THE RHINE.

Top left: Charles Wentworth Dilke. From a miniature in the possession of his great-great-grandson, Sir John Dilke.

Top right: Charles Wentworth Dilke in later life. From the painting by Arthur Hughes.

Bottom: The editor of the *Athenaeum*. This cartoon of Dilke by his friend, contributor, and host, Thomas Hood, was published in Hood's *Up the Rhine*, 1840.

Maria Dilke (1780–1850) was universally popular in the Keats circle. Keats and Brown addressed her a mock love-letter, Fanny Keats sent her 'a present of facescreens and a workbag', George offered his warm regards from Kentucky, and Fanny Brawne remained her friend for life. Maria was unpunctual and remarkably pretty. Her warmth and practical kindness, her pleasure in singing and dancing, in gossip and good food are frequently recorded. A woman of literary tastes, she was the perfect wife for Dilke. This miniature is in the possession of her great-great-grandson.

42

Opposite: 'Dilke has continually in his mouth "my Boy",' Keats wrote to his brother George in April 1819. 'This is what spoils princes: it may have the same effect with Commoners.' Dilke's only son, born in 1810, proved to be a man of distinction. With Sir Joseph Paxton and Professor Lindley, he founded *The Gardener's Chronicle*; he largely revived the Royal Horticultural Society, and botanists named an order of passion-flowers *passifloracea Dilkea*. 'Dilke's Boy' was a Member of Parliament, and Chairman of the Society of Arts; he helped to organise the Great Exhibition, and he was given a baronetcy in recognition of the Prince Consort's personal esteem for him. These achievements did not, however, satisfy his father. Dilke had seen him as a barrister; he did not forgive him for his failure to conform to the predetermined parental pattern. He gave to his grandson, the future Sir Charles Dilke, all the affection he had shown his son; he determined that the child should fulfil the ambitions which the man had disappointed. This portrait of Sir C. Wentworth Dilke, Bt. (d. 1869) was painted by Alexander Craig in about 1840.

Above left: Sir C. Wentworth Dilke, Bt. From a portrait painted in about 1850.

Above right: 'Dilke's Boy': a detail from *The Royal Commissioners for the Great Exhibition, 1851*, by Henry Windham Phillips. Dilke is the standing figure on the extreme left.

Left: Dilke's grandson, Sir Charles Dilke, Bt. (1843–1911). A Privy Councillor and Under-Secretary of State for Foreign Affairs, Dilke's political career was ruined by domestic scandal in 1885. His natural reticence was no doubt intensified by the Crawford case. He destroyed not only personal papers, but a mass of Keatsiana, 'calculated by the bushel', which he had inherited.

This portrait of Sir Charles was painted by G. F. Watts; it was shown at the Royal Academy's summer exhibition in 1880.

Right: William Dilke, the younger brother of Keats's friend, and the 'Mr. W.D.' of Keats's letters, was born on 16 August 1796; he had an eventful career as a commissary in the Peninsula, America and France. Sir Charles Dilke later wore on his keys 'my great-uncle Dilke's Peninsular medal marked with his battles'. It was William Dilke who painted the name Wentworth Place on the house in which Keats lived. He himself lived for a time in Wentworth House, which he had built across the road from Wentworth Place. He helped Sir Sidney Colvin with his life of Keats, and he died in 1885. This portrait of him was painted by Sir David Wilkie in about 1830.

Left: William Dilke. From the miniature by F. W. Wilkin: possibly a copy of the Wilkie portrait.

Right: In mid-December 1817, Keats dined with Horace Smith, and met his two brothers with 'Hill and Kingston and one Du Bois ... These men say things which make one start,' he reported to his brothers, 'without making one feel, they are all alike; their manners are alike; they all know fashionables; they have a mannerism in their very eating, in their mere handling a Decanter. They talked of Kean and his low Company. Would I were with that Company—instead of yours said I to myself!'

Edward du Bois (1774–1850) was a wit and man of letters and a judge in the Court of Requests. He wrote regularly for the *Morning Chronicle*, and edited *The Monthly Mirror*. This print of him, published by Richard Bentley in 1839, was taken from a portrait once in the possession of Thomas Hill.

45

James Elmes earns one brief missive and a reference in Keats's letters. He was born in London on 15 October 1782, and entered the Merchant Taylors' School in 1796. He later became a pupil of George Gibson, and a student at the Royal Academy, where he won a silver medal for architectural design. In 1809 he was vice-president of the London Architectural Society. He was also Surveyor of the Port of London, but his failing sight compelled him to retire in 1848. Though he designed and erected a good many buildings in London, he devoted most of his attention to the literature of art. He was the editor of Shepherd's *Metropolitan Improvements*; he wrote the first documented life of Sir Christopher Wren. He was a frequent contributor to architectural and antiquarian periodicals, and from 1816 to 1820 he was editor of *The Annals of the Fine Arts*, the first periodical work of its kind. Elmes was the loyal champion of his friend B. R. Haydon, and of the Elgin Marbles. It was through Haydon that he made the acquaintance of Keats. The odes 'To a Nightingale' and 'On a Grecian Urn', and the sonnets 'To Haydon' and 'On Seeing the Elgin Marbles', made their first appearance in the *Annals*. Elmes died at Greenwich on 2 April 1862, and was buried at Charlton. This portrait of him was painted by his friend James Lonsdale (1777–1839).

William Ewing, the ivory carver, was among the very few who saw Keats outside England. He met him in Rome, and (as Severn told Brown): 'Altho' we came here strangers to him, he gave us all the attention of an old friend.' Ewing attended Keats's funeral; later, in Hampstead, he met Fanny Brawne. 'He seemed so fluttered and confused,' she reported to Fanny Keats, 'that I could make nothing of him; but he has claims on us both from his great kindness in Italy.' Ewing is an elusive figure; the dates of his birth and death remain unknown. In 1822 he exhibited four works at the Royal Academy, including a portrait in ivory of Canova, done in Rome in 1820, and a portrait in ivory of Pope Pius VII, done in Rome in 1821. He was living as late as 1831.

Francis Fladgate (1799–1892) was a relative of James Rice, and a boon companion of Keats. For fifty-nine years he was a member of the Garrick Club; a fellow-member found him 'one of the most polished gentlemen and good-natured persons I ever met'. This portrait, at the Garrick Club, is inscribed: 'Francis Fladgate, Esq., Hon Sec. of the Garrick Club, 1849. Painted & Presented to the Garrick Club by Henry O'Neil, A.R.A.' Another picture at the Club shows Fladgate in a group of billiard-players in 1869.

Top: Harry Buxton Forman, C.B. (1842–1917). A senior civil servant in the Post Office, he rose to be controller of packet services; he also edited the *Letters of John Keats to Fanny Brawne* (1878) and *The Poetical Works and other Writings of John Keats* (1883). He has been described, with justice, as 'the first real collector and annotator of Keats's letters, whose work will never be entirely superseded'.

Bottom: 'You will be glad to hear that Gifford's attack upon me has done me service—it has got my Book among several *Sets* . . .' So Keats told his brother and sister-in-law on 17 December 1818. William Gifford (1756–1826) edited the *Quarterly Review*, which had recently published John Wilson Croker's notorious onslaught on *Endymion*. This engraving of Gifford was done by Ridley after the painting by John Hoppner.

Left: Keats presumably met George Robert Gleig (1796–1888) through Benjamin Bailey, who was later to marry Gleig's sister. Both Gleig and Bailey were undergraduates at Oxford. Gleig—the son of the Bishop of Brechin—served in the Peninsular Campaign, and wrote a vivid account of it in his novel *The Subaltern*. He was later ordained, and showed the more serious side of his nature as a historian, and as inspector-general of military schools (1846–57). He was Chaplain-General of the forces from 1844 to 1875. Keats sent him his respects and 'best regards', and referred to him several times in his letters. This engraving of Gleig was published by Henry Colburn in 1837.

Right: On Christmas Day 1817, William Godwin noted in his journal: 'Meet Keats.' The meeting was not recorded in Keats's letters, but Keats read Godwin's *Political Justice* and at least three of his novels. Godwin (1756–1836) was the father-in-law of Shelley; he was an atheist and a philosopher of anarchical views. He believed that men acted according to reason, that reason taught benevolence, and that rational creatures could live in harmony without laws and institutions. This portrait of Godwin was engraved by Roberts from a painting by Thomas Kearsley. It was published in 1821.

Joseph Henry Green (1791–1863) was a demonstrator in the dissecting room at Guy's Hospital when Keats became a medical student. He took as much interest in philosophy as in surgery, and, from 1817, he was a close friend of Coleridge, with whom Keats met him on Hampstead Heath. Green was elected surgeon to St. Thomas's Hospital; he later became Professor of Surgery at King's College, and he was twice President of the Royal College of Surgeons, which owns this portrait of him by Thomas Phillips.

Benjamin Robert Haydon was the son of a stationer in Plymouth, where he was born on 26 January 1786. In 1804 he came to London and became a student at the Royal Academy, and three years later he showed his first picture. The hanging of this and his next work led to a quarrel between the artist and the authorities, and Haydon's arrogance and impulsiveness led him to quarrel with patrons, friends and critics for the rest of his life. He was a powerful propagandist, a good writer and an excellent lecturer, and he succeeded in making the nation buy the Elgin Marbles; his journal is a fascinating psychological document. But he had chosen to devote himself to the lost cause of historical painting; and after a lifetime of struggle he shot himself on 22 June 1846.

Cowden Clarke introduced Keats to Haydon in 1816. Keats welcomed the introduction to 'this glorious Haydon and all his creation'. He addressed a sonnet to him, and wrote two more when they had visited the newly acquired Elgin Marbles. Haydon confessed himself his 'ardent friend'. Keats visited his studio and, on 28 December 1817, with Lamb and Wordsworth and others, he attended Haydon's Immortal Dinner. The friendship was embittered when Haydon refused to repay a loan, but Keats attended the private exhibition of Haydon's picture 'Christ's Entry into Jerusalem', in which his own face appeared with those of Wordsworth, Lamb and Hazlitt. Haydon called on him several times during his last months in England.

Keats himself drew 'a vile caricature of B. R. Haydon' (*left*), and Haydon painted this self-portrait, which is now in the National Portrait Gallery.

Left: 'There are three things to rejoice at in this Age,' Keats wrote to Haydon in 1818: 'The Excursion, Your Pictures, and Hazlitt's depth of Taste.' Keats attended Hazlitt's lectures on English poetry, dined with him at Haydon's and at Hessey's, and often referred to meetings with him. This drawing of William Hazlitt (1788–1830) was made by William Bewick in 1825.

Right: James Augustus Hessey was born on 28 August 1785, with 'very genteel and wealthy Connexions'. As a young man, he seems to have run away from his family in Yorkshire, and by 1803 he was working for Lackington & Company: the London publishers in whose offices he met John Taylor. In 1806 Taylor & Hessey established themselves as booksellers and publishers at 93, Fleet Street, and by April 1817 they had become the publishers of Keats. 'Mistessey,' as Keats called him, showed his admiration and affectionate concern for the poet, but he was less close to him than his partner; this may have owed something to the fact that Taylor remained a bachelor, while Hessey married Kate Falkner and led his own domestic life. In 1821 Taylor and Hessey bought the *London Magazine*, and under their aegis it became one of the finest of English literary periodicals; but later issues deteriorated, the firm was losing money, and in 1825 Taylor and Hessey regretfully dissolved their partnership. In 1829 Hessey went bankrupt, but he soon established himself again, in Regent Street, as a bookseller and auctioneer. By July 1834 he was headmaster of a Hampstead school, at which two of Taylor's nephews were pupils. He remained on the warmest terms with Taylor himself. In 1861 he moved to Wiltshire, where he died on 7 April 1870.

This drawing of Hessey was possibly a sketch for the portrait which William Hilton painted in about 1817.

Above: Mr. and Mrs. James Augustus Hessey (from contemporary silhouettes).

Opposite top: Thomas Hill (1760–1840): book collector, part proprietor of *The Monthly Mirror,* and one of the mannered company Keats met when he dined with Horace Smith in mid-December 1817. This engraving was made after a painting by John Linnell.

Opposite bottom: William Hilton, born in Lincoln in 1786, is mentioned only three times in Keats's letters, but—like his brother-in-law, De Wint—he knew him better than might be supposed. He made a 'fine, if too precise, chalk drawing' of the poet, and he contributed towards his expenses in Italy. He also painted the posthumous portrait based on Severn's miniature. A distinguished historical painter, Hilton became a Royal Academician in 1818, and Keeper in 1827. He died on 30 December 1839. The *Athenaeum* reported that '... his death was occasioned by the asthma, and by the strength of his affections; for he never recovered [from] the loss of a beloved wife some years since. Though his frame was attenuated by sickness and sorrow, he retained the lustre of genius in his eye, and its brightness on his expansive forehead, to the last. His manners were singularly amiable and pleasing ... He died regretted, respected, and admired by all who could appreciate mental and moral excellence in union.'

This self-portrait of Hilton is in the Usher Gallery, Lincoln.

THOMAS HILL, ESQ:

Left: On 11 February 1818 Mary Shelley wrote in her journal: 'Spend the evening at Hunt's', and Claire Clairmont added in her diary: 'Peacock, Hogg, and Keats were present.' This silhouette of Thomas Jefferson Hogg (1792–1862), the friend and biographer of Shelley, was cut in 1810, when he was an undergraduate at Oxford.

Right: Thomas Hood (1799–1845) married into the Keats circle when he became the husband of Jane Reynolds. This portrait of him was painted at Lake House, Wanstead, by William Hilton, between 1832 and 1834.

Opposite: James Henry Leigh Hunt was born on 19 October 1784, and educated at Christ's Hospital. In 1808 he began to edit *The Examiner*; and in 1813, with his brother John, he was fined and imprisoned for a libel on the Prince Regent. This pencil drawing was made by Thomas Charles Wageman in February 1815, when Hunt had just served his sentence at Coldbath Fields. Keats marked his release with the sonnet 'Written on the day that Mr. Leigh Hunt left prison'. Keats was later introduced to Hunt, and often visited his Hampstead cottage; Hunt brought about his meeting with Shelley, and recognised them both as poets of genius. Keats soon outgrew Hunt's influence, but they remained good friends, and Keats lived briefly with him in the summer of 1820. Hunt was a gifted essayist and a wide-ranging critic; but, for all his writing and editing, his difficult wife and his numerous children forced him to live a life of 'poetical tinkerdom'. He died on 28 August 1859.

Leigh Hunt

Leigh Hunt. From a silhouette by his wife, Marianne Hunt.

Left: 'The Edinburgh review are affraid to touch upon my Poem,' Keats wrote to his brother and sister-in-law in September 1819. '... The Cowardliness of the Edinburgh is worse than the abuse of the Quarterly.' Francis Jeffrey, the editor of the *Edinburgh Review*, did not discuss *Endymion* until he reviewed the *Lamia* volume in August 1820. 'We do not know any book,' he decided, 'which we would sooner employ as a test to ascertain whether any one had in him a native relish for poetry.' Charles Brown considered that these comments came 'too late for a good purpose'. Keats was about to leave for Italy. This portrait of Francis Jeffrey, Lord Jeffrey (1773–1850), was painted by A. Geddes in 1826.

Right: 'I saw Kean return to the public in Richard III, and finely he did it,' wrote Keats to his brothers on 21 December 1817. He much admired the actor, and hoped (though in vain) to see him in 'the hotblooded character of Ludolph' in the play which he wrote with Brown: *Otho the Great.* Edmund Kean (1787–1833) is seen here as Richard III, in the painting by John James Halls (1814).

Fanny Keats, the poet's only sister, was born on 3 June 1803. Her parents died when she was very young; and, after the death of her grandmother, Mrs. Jennings, in December 1814, she went to live with her guardian, Richard Abbey, and his wife at Walthamstow. Her brothers rarely saw her, but Keats wrote her some of his most engaging and affectionate letters, and tried his best to lighten her isolation. After his departure for Italy, she became a close friend of Fanny Brawne; in 1826 she married a Spanish diplomat and man of letters, Valentin Maria Llanos y Gutierrez. The rest of her long life was spent largely in Spain. She remained devoted to her brother's memory. She helped Harry Buxton Forman to edit the letters of Keats; she proudly refused to sell the letters which Keats had sent her. These were given to the British Museum after her death on 16 December 1889.

This portrait of Fanny Llanos was recently discovered by her great-great-grandson, Dr. Fernando Paradinas. It shows her at an earlier age than any other likeness so far seen.

Top: Fanny Llanos. From a portrait painted in middle age.

Bottom: Fanny Llanos. This picture was found in Spain a few months ago. The artist is probably her son, Juan.

Valentin Maria Llanos y Gutierrez (1796?–1885). This photograph, coloured and mounted, was recently found among family papers. Taken in Rome, it is clearly the companion to the familiar photograph (*opposite*) of his wife. This was taken in Rome in 1863, when she was sixty.

Above: Valentin Llanos and his wife. These hitherto unpublished photographs were also taken in Rome in 1863.

Opposite: Portrait of Fanny Llanos by her son, Juan Llanos. Presented by her to Harry Buxton Forman, and by Mrs. Buxton Forman to Keats House, Hampstead.

Fanny Llanos in old age. From a portrait in the possession of Dr. Ernesto Paradinas.

Valentin Llanos: the companion portrait. On 10 October 1885 the *Athenaeum* announced: 'We have received from Spain intelligence of the death of Señor Valentin Llanos, the brother-in-law of John Keats, and author of two romances which attracted some attention in their day, namely, "Don Esteban" and "Sandoval the Freemason". Señor Llanos was in his ninetieth year, and was free from any specific disease when he passed away in his sleep on the 14th of August. His widow, the Fanny Keats to whom so many charming brotherly letters were written by the poet in the first quarter of the present century, retains, at the age of eighty-two, her mental and bodily vigour, though somewhat shaken by her loss. Mr. Llanos, who was a man of much refinement and scholarship, has left among his papers an English version of the "Gran Galeotto" of Echegaray, and a three-volume manuscript (also in English) entitled "The Spanish Exile", dealing with English manners of sixty years since in the form of a novel.'

67

Juan and Rosa Llanos, son and daughter of Fanny Keats. In the first of these photographs, taken in about 1890, Severn's miniature of their 'uncle Keats' may be seen on the wall. In the second photograph they are seated under the portraits of their parents.

George Keats, the poet's younger brother, was born on 28 February 1797. He was educated with him at Enfield, and worked for a while in the offices of their guardian, Richard Abbey. 'George has ever been more than a brother to me, he has been my greatest friend,' wrote Keats in 1818. That year George married Georgiana Augusta Wylie, and emigrated with her to America. In January 1820 he paid a brief business visit to London; he left his brother with little money, and his behaviour remained a subject of bitter contention in the Keats circle. George did not visit England again. He established himself as a leading citizen and businessman in Louisville, Kentucky, and he became the father of two sons and six daughters. He died on 24 December 1841; in 1843 his widow married a Scottish engineer, John Jeffrey. She died on 3 April 1879, being nearly eighty at her death.

This watercolour miniature of George Keats was painted by Joseph Severn. It was presented to the Keats–Shelley Memorial House in Rome by the granddaughters of George Keats, the daughters of Emma Keats Speed.

George and Georgiana Keats. From silhouettes cut in about 1830.

71

This life-mask, the most haunting likeness of Keats, was made by Benjamin Robert Haydon in 1816, when the poet was twenty-one. Fanny Llanos assured Harry Buxton Forman that it was 'a perfect copy of the features of my dear brother'. Sending him a sketch of it, she added: 'It is perfect, except for the mouth, the lips being rather thicker and somewhat more compressed which renders the expression more severe than the sweet and mild original.'

Top: A page from Haydon's journal, November 1816, showing a sketch for the portrait of Keats in Haydon's painting, 'Christ's Entry into Jerusalem.'

Bottom: John Keats. This charcoal drawing by Joseph Severn (1816) is his earliest known drawing of Keats done from the life. It is 'by far the best likeness' of him, Severn assured Buxton Forman in 1877.

John Keats. From the silhouette by Charles Armitage Brown, *c.* January 1819.

John Keats, by Joseph Severn, 1819. From the original miniature in the
National Portrait Gallery. A replica, also by Severn, was once owned by Jane
Reynolds (Mrs. Thomas Hood). It is now at Keats House, Hampstead. A
further replica belonged to Fanny Brawne. Towards the end of her life she
was compelled by financial troubles to sell it to C. W. Dilke; his grandson, Sir
Charles Dilke, presented it to the Keats–Shelley Memorial House in Rome.

'If Brown would take a little of my advice, he could not fail to be the first pallet of his day.' So Keats assured Dilke on 31 July 1819. Brown made this pencil sketch of Keats that summer in the Isle of Wight. It is the most accomplished of his drawings.

John Keats. From the silhouette by Mrs. Leigh Hunt.

Left: '28 Janry 3 o'clock mng. Drawn to keep me awake—a deadly sweat was on him all this night.' So Severn inscribed this drawing of Keats, which was done less than a month before his death (23 February 1821). Charles Cowden Clarke considered it 'a marvellously correct likeness'.

Right: 'I should like the window to open onto the Lake of Geneva—and there I'd sit and read all day like the picture of somebody reading.' So Keats wrote to his sister on 13 March 1819. This picture of him reading in his room at Wentworth Place was painted by Joseph Severn, in Rome, in 1821–2. The portrait of Shakespeare on the wall had been given to Keats by his landlady at Carisbrooke in April 1817. The details of the room were sent to Severn by Charles Brown, who was still living at Wentworth Place when the picture was painted. This authentic recollection of Keats was presented to the National Portrait Gallery in 1859: three years after the Gallery was founded.

Keats, by Patrick MacDowell, 9 September 1828. This plaster bust is said to
have been made under the supervision of Fanny Keats (then Fanny Llanos)
and Fanny Brawne.

This medallion of Keats by Giuseppe Girometti was, like the Hilton portrait, commissioned by Richard Woodhouse. It was intended as the centrepiece of a memorial, but the project did not materialise. Woodhouse gave a copy of the medallion to Brown; and, writing to Severn in the autumn of 1832, Brown said: 'The bas-relief he gave me of our Keats delights me; never was anything so like, it seems quite a piece of magic.'

Keats listening to the nightingale on Hampstead Heath. This impression of
him was painted by Joseph Severn in 1845: nearly a quarter-century after the
poet's death.

Tom Keats was born on 18 November 1799. The youngest surviving brother of Keats, he was said by George to have understood him better than anyone. Like his brothers, he went to Mr. Clarke's school at Enfield. He worked for a while in Mr. Abbey's office in Pancras Lane, but ill-health obliged him to leave. His brothers gave him touching care. George went with him to France and to Devonshire, Keats stayed with him in Devonshire and Kent; but tuberculosis had taken hold. In August 1818 Dilke was obliged to summon Keats back from Scotland; and for the next few weeks Keats nursed 'poor Tom who looks upon me as his only comfort'. Tom died on 1 December, a few days after his nineteenth birthday.

This watercolour miniature was painted by Joseph Severn in the year of Tom's death. It was given by John Gilmer Speed, a son-in-law of George Keats, to the Keats–Shelley Memorial House in Rome.

CHARLES LAMB,

From a Drawing by Hancock (1798) in the Possession of Mr Cottle.

Charles Lamb (1775–1834). Poet, letter-writer and essayist, he is best known as the author of the *Essays of Elia*. Keats met him at Haydon's Immortal Dinner on 28 December 1817, and probably saw him more often than the letters suggest. Writing to his brother George in the autumn of 1819, he told him: 'The though[t] of you[r] little girl puts me in mind of a thing I heard a Mr Lamb say. A child in arms was passing by his chair towards the mother, in the nurses arms. Lamb took hold of the long clothes saying "Where, god bless me, where does it leave off?" '

83

On 12 July 1820 Mrs. Gisborne noted in her journal: 'We drank tea at Mr Hunt's; I was much pained by the sight of poor Keats, under sentence of death from Dr. Lamb.' William Lambe was the son of Lacon Lambe, an attorney practising at Warwick. He is said to have been born at Warwick on 26 February 1765, but the register of St. John's College, Cambridge, gives Hereford as his county of birth. In 1782 he was admitted to St. John's; in 1788 he was admitted Foundress Fellow, and he continued to live in college, pursuing the study of medicine, until his marriage in 1794. He then vacated his fellowship and went to live in Warwick, where he succeeded to the practice of Dr. Landor, father of Walter Savage Landor. Eventually he moved to London, where in 1804 he became a Fellow of the Royal College of Physicians. In 1805 he published *A medical and experimental inquiry into the origin of Constitutional diseases, particularly Scrofula, Consumption, Cancer and Gout*. At about the time he settled in London he became a strict vegetarian, and in 1809 he produced a book to show that almost all diseases had their origin in the use of animal diet, and in the impure water supplied in the metropolis. In London, Lambe came to know the Shelleys; he also met Dr. George Darling, who called him in to examine Keats in the summer of 1820. It was on their joint advice that Keats went to Italy. It is recorded that Dr. Lambe 'had never any considerable practice of a remunerative character, and lived for many years a short distance out of town. He had, however, a consulting-room in King's road, Bedford-row, at which he was in the habit of attending three times a week. Never was a poor patient turned from the door at any of the hours of his attendance, and this most benevolent man assisted with money those who without it were unable to obtain the little luxuries necessary in sickness and the medicines he had prescribed.' He died on 11 June 1847 at Dilwyn, in Herefordshire, where he is buried.

The silhouette of William Lambe shows him at the age of twenty-two; the second likeness, taken from a daguerreotype, shows him when he was over eighty years old.

'I went last Tuesday, an hour too late, to Hazlitt's Lecture on poetry, got there just as they were coming out, when all these pounced upon me—Hazlitt, John Hunt and Son, Wells, Bewick, all the Landseers...' So Keats told his brothers on 23 January 1818. 'All the Landseers' would include John (1769–1852) and his sons Thomas (1795–1880), Charles (1799–1879) and Edwin (1802–73). John is portrayed here by Edwin (1843).

Thomas Landseer largely devoted his life to etching the works of his brother Edwin; elected A.R.A. in 1868, he published a life of William Bewick in 1871. This coloured chalk and stump portrait of Thomas (*left*) was drawn by his brother Charles. Charles himself was recorded in pen and ink by Solomon Alexander Hart in the 1840s (*top*). Edwin entered the Royal Academy schools in 1816, and began to exhibit the following year. He gradually established himself with his animal pictures as perhaps the most popular painter of the age. He designed the lions for Nelson's Column in Trafalgar Square. He drew this self-portrait (*bottom*) in 1818.

'I did not mention that I had seen the British Gallery,' Keats wrote to his brothers on 21 February 1818. '... I could not bear Leslie's Uriel.' Keats knew Charles Robert Leslie, R.A. (1794–1859). William Holl did this engraving of Leslie after an early self-portrait.

John Gibson Lockhart (1794–1854). The son-in-law of Sir Walter Scott, Lockhart was known as 'the Scorpion' on account of his fierceness as a critic. Under the pseudonym 'Z' he wrote a savage attack on Keats in *Blackwood's Edinburgh Magazine*, August 1818. This portrait of him was painted by Sir Francis Grant.

Left: John Martin—Johnny Martin, as Keats called him—was born in 1791. He was a partner in Rodwell & Martin, publishers and booksellers. He drank claret with Keats at Wentworth Place, and played cards with him at Shanklin in the summer of 1819. He was a friend of Reynolds, Rice and Bailey, and a constant visitor to Little Britain. Martin retired early from business, became librarian at Woburn Abbey in 1836, and Fellow of the Society of Antiquaries. He died in 1855. This picture of him was presented by his grandson to Harry Buxton Forman.

Right: George Felton Mathew, a mercer's son, was born in London in 1795. 'My intimacy with [Keats],' he told Milnes, 'was not of long duration . . . It will always be a great pleasure to me, however, to remember that I at any time contributed to the happiness of his short life by introducing him to my father's family, and exercising towards him hospitable attentions.' Mathew was a poet, and the leader of a poetic circle; Keats addressed an epistle to him which (said the recipient) had 'many beauties'. This silhouette shows Mathew in youth.

In 1833, just down from Cambridge, Richard Monckton Milnes was making a grand tour of the Continent. He was one of the earliest and the most fervent students of Keats; and, though the collected poems had not then been published in England, he and his friends had, at their own expense, reprinted *Adonais*. In Rome, Monckton Milnes met Severn, who, he wrote, 'satisfied much of my curiosity respecting a man, whom the gods had favoured with great genius and early death'. In Florence, Milnes fell ill of malaria, and W. S. Landor took him into the Villa Gherardesca. It was there that he met 'Mr. Charles Brown, a retired Russia-merchant, with whose name I was already familiar as the generous protector and devoted friend of the Poet.' The meeting was to be significant. In 1841, on the eve of emigrating to New Zealand, Brown offered Monckton Milnes the task of establishing Keats's fame. Milnes accepted immediately. Brown sent him 'all his collection of Keats's writings, accompanied with a biographical notice, and I engaged to use them,' wrote Milnes, 'to the best of my ability.' In 1848 he published the historic *Life, Letters and Literary Remains of John Keats*. He was the first to champion Keats as a poet of genius. This photograph of Richard Monckton Milnes, first Baron Houghton (1809–85) was taken in later life.

On 15 April 1819 Keats reported to his brother and sister-in-law: 'I went with Hunt to Sir John Leicester's gallery, there I saw Northcote— Hilton—Bewick and many more...' This engraving of James Northcote (1746–1831), Royal Academician and author, was made, after his self-portrait, by H. Meyer, and published in 1815.

Vincent Novello (1781–1861) was a celebrated organist and composer, and father-in-law of Cowden Clarke. Keats used to visit Novello at 240, Oxford Street—'the Land of Harpsicols', he called it; but in time he grew weary of the company. 'The night we went to Novello's,' he told his brother George, in December 1818, 'there was a complete set to of Mozart and punning—I was so completely tired of it that if I were to follow my own inclinations I should never meet any one of that set again.'

This painting of the Novello family circle in about 1830 was done by Edward Novello. From left to right: Charles Cowden Clarke stands holding some music, and Mary Cowden Clarke sits in front of him. Vincent Novello is playing, Edward Novello can be seen in profile, and Mrs. Vincent Novello is sitting on the extreme right of the picture. Behind Vincent Novello stands Edward Holmes (1797–1859), who had been a schoolfriend of Keats at Enfield. Apprenticed to a bookseller, he later chose the profession of music, and studied under Vincent Novello, who took him into his household for several years.

On 11 February 1818, Keats spent the evening at Leigh Hunt's. Among those present was Thomas Love Peacock (1785–1866). Peacock was an official of the East India Company, a poet, and the author of satirical novels, among them *Headlong Hall* (1816) and *Nightmare Abbey* (1818). This miniature of him was painted by Roger Jean in about 1805.

Left: George Reynolds (1764?–1853) was born in London, and became a pupil at Christ's Hospital. For several years he taught at Shrewsbury; in 1806 he returned to London, where he became master of the Lambeth Boys' Parochial School, writing master to the Female Asylum, Lambeth, and writing master to Christ's Hospital from 1817 to 1835. He and his wife eventually settled in Little Britain with their son, John Hamilton Reynolds, and their four daughters. At the height of his friendship with Reynolds, Keats was a frequent visitor. This sketch is the only known likeness of the master of the house.

Right: Mrs. George Reynolds—*née* Charlotte Cox—was born in 1761 and died in 1848. A devoted wife and mother, she was also a woman of literary tastes, and, under the pen-name of Mrs. Hamerton, she published a story, *Mrs. Leslie and Her Grandchildren*, which earned the warm approval of Charles Lamb. Keats promised her a bound copy of *Endymion*, and wrote a sonnet 'To Mrs. Reynolds's Cat'. Mrs. Reynolds's niece, Jane Cox, was the Charmian who enthralled him in September 1818. This portrait of Mrs. Reynolds, the only known likeness of her, was painted by William Hilton, at the Hoods' house in Wanstead, between 1832 and 1834.

Jane Reynolds (Mrs. Thomas Hood) was a 'dear friend' of Keats. Perhaps she felt more than affection for him, for she expressed her dislike of Fanny Brawne, and in September 1819 he wrote that, J. H. Reynolds apart, he was 'p[r]ejudiced against all that family'. No doubt Keats had Jane Reynolds in mind when he wrote to Fanny Brawne of 'these Laughers, who do not like you, who envy you for your Beauty, who would have God-bless'd me from you for ever'. In 1825 Jane married Thomas Hood; despite financial problems and Hood's persistent ill-health, the marriage was very happy, and Jane survived her husband only a year. This portrait of Jane Reynolds, Mrs. Thomas Hood, by an unknown artist, was painted in about 1832–4, at the same time as those of her mother and husband.

Above: Jane Reynolds (Mrs. Thomas Hood). From a silhouette.

Opposite: John Hamilton Reynolds was born in Shrewsbury on 9 September 1794. He went to Shrewsbury School and in 1806, after his family had moved to London, he entered St. Paul's School. In 1810 he became a clerk at the Amicable Insurance Office; but he was always torn between his need to earn a living and his affection for literature and the theatre. *Safie, An Eastern Tale* (1814) was admired by Byron; but Reynolds's future wife, Eliza Powell Drewe, persuaded him to be a solicitor. He proved to be unsuccessful in law; and, despite his poems, his work for the theatre and his contributions to magazines, including the *London Magazine* and the *Athenaeum*, he did not fulfil himself as a writer. In 1847 he was appointed assistant clerk of the County Court at Newport, in the Isle of Wight. His drunken habits are said to have set him beyond the social pale. He died on 15 November 1852. On his tombstone at Church Litten are inscribed the words: 'Friend of Keats'.

He had indeed been the poet's friend. In September 1817, Keats had already thought of him as a brother. Reynolds is said to have introduced him to Brown, Rice, Bailey, Taylor, Hessey, and others. He discussed poetry with him, and he reviewed *Poems* (1817) in the *Champion*; he largely counteracted the influence of Hunt. He urged Keats to write *Isabella*, and he prevented him from publishing the original reckless preface to *Endymion*. Leigh Hunt had predicted that, with Keats and Shelley, Reynolds was a poet of the future. He was, perhaps, the most tragic friend of Keats, for he was a fitful light that failed.

This miniature of J. H. Reynolds, on ivory, was painted by Joseph Severn in 1818. It belonged to Reynolds's sister, Marianne.

97

Left: John Hamilton Reynolds. From a silhouette.

Right: Mrs. J. H. Reynolds (*née* Eliza Powell Drewe). From a silhouette.

98

'She was a very beautiful girl,' wrote Dilke of John Hamilton Reynolds's sister, Marianne. '[She was] somewhat cold and saturnine, and though always admired not generally liked. She was afterwards hardly tried by misfortune, and never yielded—indeed I never thought so highly of her until she had undergone those trials, which I think were beyond the strength of any other in the family. She was never abased by them—never complained.' Marriann, as Keats called her, was born in 1797; jilted by Benjamin Bailey, she married Henry Gibson Green, and became the mother of the artists Charles and Towneley Green. She died in 1874. This pen-and-ink sketch gives some impression of her.

Left: James Rice, born in 1792, is among the most endearing and least known characters in the Keats circle. Dilke recalled 'dear generous noble James Rice' as 'the best, and in his quaint way one of the wittiest and wisest men I ever knew'. Keats delighted in his company, stayed with him in the Isle of Wight, and found him 'the most sensible, and even wise Man' of his acquaintance. Rice was educated for the law; but he suffered all his life from ill-health, and he died in 1832, at the age of forty. This watercolour miniature is now at Keats House.

Right: James Rice. From a silhouette miniature.

'Mr Robinson a great friend of Coleridge's called on me.' So Keats told his brothers on 14 February 1818. Henry Crabb Robinson did not mention the visit in his published journal, but he earns his place here as an associate member of Keats's circle. Born in 1775, he became a foreign correspondent of *The Times*, and its special correspondent in the Peninsula in 1808–9. He was afterwards a barrister. One of the founders of the Athenaeum Club and of University College London, he knew many notable people of his day. They are illuminated in the published part of his diary and correspondence. He died in 1867. This drawing of him was done by J. J. Masquerier (1778–1855).

Above: The Severn family miniature. It was painted in 1820 by Joseph Severn, who took it with him to Rome. His father and mother are seen on the right, then his sisters and brothers in order of age: Charlotte, Sarah, Maria, Tom with his hands on the keys of a harpsichord, and Charles.

Opposite: 'I know you don't like John Scott,' wrote Brown to Keats on 21 December 1820. Keats still assumed, no doubt, that Scott had written the malicious articles on the Cockney School of Poetry in *Blackwood's Edinburgh Magazine*. They are now known to have been the work of J. G. Lockhart. John Scott—who became the editor of the *London Magazine*—was mortally wounded in a duel in 1821. This drawing of him was done by Seymour Kirkup in Rome in 1819.

Left: Joseph Severn, the son of a musician, was born at Hoxton on 7 December 1793. At an early age he showed a taste for drawing, and his father apprenticed him to an engraver. Severn wanted to be a painter, and he contrived to attend the school of the Royal Academy. In 1817 he won a gold medal from the Academy for his picture 'The Cave of Despair'. In 1820, at Haslam's suggestion, he went with Keats to Rome; he was not perhaps the ideal companion for the dying poet, but he attended him with devotion. After Keats's death he remained in Rome, where his painting was accepted for the sake of the man he had served so well. In 1861 he became British Consul in Rome, an appointment which he held for eleven years. He continued to recall Keats, in print and on canvas, until his death on 3 August 1879. He was buried beside Keats in the Protestant Cemetery. Severn drew this self-portrait in pencil when he was twenty-nine.

Right: Joseph Severn. From a drawing made by John Partridge in Rome in November 1825.

In 1828 Severn married Elizabeth, the daughter of General Lord Archibald
Montgomerie (who had died in 1814), and the ward of his patroness, Lady
Westmorland. There were six children of the marriage. Mrs. Severn died at
Marseilles in April, 1862. This watercolour portrait of her was painted by
her daughter Mary in 1851.

Joseph Severn is the central figure in this photograph. It is the only known actual likeness of him. It was taken in Italy in 1872, when he was seventy-nine.

Joseph Severn in his consular uniform. He began this self-portrait in 1876, when he was just eighty-three.

Keats met Shelley at Leigh Hunt's, but perhaps the difference in their social backgrounds made him uncomfortable in Shelley's presence, and made him afraid that Shelley would patronise him. He could never be a close friend. Shelley expressed his sympathy for Keats by inviting him to live with him in Pisa; he expressed his admiration, and his sense of loss at Keats's death, in *Adonais*. This portrait of Percy Bysshe Shelley (1792–1822) was painted by Amelia Curran in 1819.

'Does Mrs S. cut Bread and Butter as neatly as ever?' Keats asked Hunt on 10 May 1817. 'Tell her to procure some fatal Scissors and cut the thread of Life of all to be disappointed Poets.' When Keats was about to leave for Italy in 1820, Shelley wrote to him: 'Mrs Shelley unites with myself in urging the request, that you would take up your residence with us.' This portrait of Mary Shelley (1797–1851), daughter of William Godwin, second wife of Shelley, and author of *Frankenstein*, was painted by Richard Rothwell in 1841.

Horatio (Horace) Smith (1779–1849) was the brother of James Smith (1775–1839), and the author, with him, of *Rejected Addresses*, which appeared in 1812. In mid-December 1817 Keats 'dined with Horace Smith and met his two brothers with Hill and Kingston and one Du Bois, they only served to convince me,' he wrote, 'how superior humour is to wit in respect to enjoyment . . . I know such like acquaintance will never do for me.' Early in 1818, however, Keats assured Horace Smith that he was 'greatly amused' by his poem 'Nehemiah Muggs', and he refused an invitation from him with apparent regret. A year later he delightedly quoted one of Smith's witticisms.

Henry Stephens receives only one passing reference in Keats's letters, yet he
had known him since they were both medical students at the united hospitals
of Guy's and St. Thomas's, perhaps as early as 1815. They had shared rooms
in St. Thomas's Street, and, in Stephens' words, they were 'constant Com-
panions'. They met for the last time on 22 June 1818, when Stephens was in
practice at Redbourne, on the Hertfordshire border. Keats, passing through
with his brother George, his new sister-in-law, and Charles Brown, invited
him to meet them at the inn. Stephens later contributed his recollections of
Keats to the *Life and Letters* by Richard Monckton Milnes.

111

When Keats sent Taylor some lines from *Lamia*, on 5 September 1819, he wrote to him at 'Mr. James Taylor's/Retford/Notts.' There is no evidence that he ever met Taylor's father, a Retford bookseller, but James Taylor, senior, was well aware of Keats. It was to him that John Taylor had announced in 1817: 'We have agreed for the next Edit. of Keats's Poems and are to have the refusal of his future Works. I cannot think he will fail to become a great Poet.' This watercolour portrait of James Taylor (1752–1823) was painted by William Hilton.

John Taylor, son of James, was born at East Retford, in Nottingham-shire, on 31 July 1781. At the age of eighteen he went to London, where he worked for a publisher and met James Augustus Hessey, his future partner and lifelong friend. In 1806 they established their own firm at 93, Fleet Street, where their rooms became the haunt of Lamb, De Quincey, Barry Cornwall, and several of the Keats circle. By 15 April 1817 Taylor & Hessey had become the publishers of Keats. Taylor was convinced from the first of his genius. He was also deeply attached to the man. 'If you knew him,' he told a correspondent, 'you would also feel that strange personal Interest in all that concerns him.' He published *Endymion* and the *Lamia* volume of 1820. He gave Keats professional advice, affectionate encouragement and finan-cial help. He was, indeed, the perfect publisher. In 1821 he and Hessey bought the *London Magazine*, which Taylor edited with distinction. In 1825 financial pressures forced them to dissolve their partnership. Taylor became publisher to the new London University, retired in 1853, and died on 5 July 1864. This portrait by William Hilton was painted in about 1817.

114

Opposite top: John Taylor, by Joseph Severn.

Opposite bottom: John Taylor. From a drawing by an unknown artist.

Above: John Taylor. From a medallion (artist unknown).

115

John Taylor in later life. This daguerreotype, the only known actual likeness of Keats's publisher, was taken by Antoine Claudet, who had purchased from Daguerre a licence to operate in England. The outside case of the daguerreotype bears the Royal Arms, presumably because Claudet held a Royal Warrant; a further inscription on the case reads: '107, Regent's Street Quadrant.' Since Claudet did not use the Arms until 1859, one may date this likeness between 1859 and 1864, the year of Taylor's death.

On 27 April 1818, from Teignmouth, Keats reported to John Hamilton Reynolds: 'Tom has taken a fancy to a physician here, Dr Turton, and I think is getting better—therefore I shall perhaps remain here some Months.' William Turton had been born at Olveston, in Gloucestershire, on 21 May 1762, the fifth child of a local solicitor. In 1791 he had graduated as Bachelor of Medicine at Oxford. He was not only a practising physician but a notable conchologist. In 1809 he had been elected a Fellow of the Linnean Society, and in 1819 he produced *A Conchological Dictionary of the British Islands*. On the title-page is a double profile of Dr. Turton, formed by the edges of a design of a vase and stand; it is the only known likeness of the author. Dr. Turton died in Bideford on 28 December 1835, but he had earned his place in Keats's letters. His collection of shells is now in the National Museum at Washington; and *Turtonia*, a genus of bivalve shells, was named in his honour in 1849.

117

Writing to his brother and sister-in-law in February 1819, Keats told them: 'The only time I went out from Bedhampton was to see a Chapel consecrated ... This Chapel is built by a Mr Way a great Jew converter—who in that line has spent one hundred thousand Pounds.' The consecration had taken place on 25 January. Lewis Way (1772–1840) had come into a fortune, and in 1817 he had given up the law to become a priest. He had spent his money lavishly on others, and he had been rewarded with gibes from Macaulay and Praed. This watercolour of Lewis Way, by Mrs. Poole, is at Merton College, Oxford.

Left: Charles Jeremiah Wells (*c.* 1800–79) was a schoolfriend of Tom Keats, and Keats himself addressed a sonnet to him. 'Wells and Severn dined with me yesterday,' he told his brothers on 5 January 1818. 'We had a very pleasant day—I pitched upon another bottle of claret—Port—we enjoyed ourselves very much were all very witty and full of Rhyme.' Wells was engaging but untrustworthy; he sent Tom a series of letters purporting to come from a girl, Amena, who was desperately in love with him. Keats considered that the hoax had had an adverse effect on Tom's health. After Tom's death he found 'some of the correspondence between him and that degraded Wells and Amena—It is a wretched business.' He broke with Wells for good. This miniature of Wells was painted by Thomas Charles Wageman.

Right: On 24 May 1818 Keats dined with Hazlitt, Barnes and Wilkie at Haydon's. This likeness of Sir David Wilkie (1785–1841), painter of portraits and *genre* pictures, shows him as he was in his youth.

Richard Woodhouse, the eldest in a family of fourteen children, was born in Bath on 11 December 1788; his father later owned the White Hart Inn, and he seems, besides, to have been a man of literary tastes. Richard was educated at Eton; unlike some of his brothers, he did not go to Oxford or Cambridge, but in 1815, after a protracted stay in Spain and Portugal, he published *A Grammar of the Spanish, Portuguese, and Italian Languages*. He had already turned to the law, and—working in the Temple—he had become a literary and legal adviser to Taylor and Hessey. It was in their offices, at 93, Fleet Street, that he first met Keats.

'Whatever People regret that they could not do for Shakespeare or Chatterton, because he did not live in their time, that I would embody into a Rational principle, and (with due regard to certain expediencies) do for Keats.' So Woodhouse wrote in 1819. He put his beliefs into practice. He was not only a wise and farsighted critic, but a generous, practical friend and a devoted Boswell. He copied out Keats's poems; he commissioned Hilton to paint his portrait, and Girometti to sculpt his medallion. He cherished Keats during his lifetime, and he played a crucial part in the development of his fame. Woodhouse died of tuberculosis on 3 September 1834, and he was buried in the Temple Church.

The only known likeness of Woodhouse is this oil painting, by an unknown artist, which shows him in boyhood.

'I am sorry that Wordsworth has left a bad impression where-ever he visited in town by his egotism, Vanity, and bigotry. Yet he is a great poet if not a philosopher.' So Keats told his brothers on 21 February 1818. He himself had seen 'a great deal' of Wordsworth in London; he had met him at Haydon's Immortal Dinner, and he apparently forgave him for dismissing the 'Hymn to Pan', in *Endymion*, as 'a pretty piece of Paganism'. Keats had also met Wordsworth's 'beautiful Wife and his enchanting Sister'. This watercolour of William Wordsworth (1770–1850) and his wife, Mary, was painted by Margaret Gillies in 1839. The other portrait shows Wordsworth's sister and constant companion, Dorothy (1771–1855).

PICTURE
ACKNOWLEDGEMENTS

Lady Birkenhead and G. Severn, Esq.: pp. 105, 107
D. Carr Taylor, Esq.: p. 113
T. J. Cartwright-Taylor, Esq.: p. 114 (bottom)
R. W. P. Cockerton, Esq.: pp. 112, 116
Sir John Dilke: pp. 40 (left), 41, 43 (left), 44
La Contessa Gigliucci: pp. 32 (both), 92
K. Guichard, Esq.: p. 45
Mrs. G. D. Hessell: p. 94 (right)
Miss Ella Keats Whiting: pp. 70, 71
T. P. F. Miller, Esq.: p. 37
Dr. Ernesto Paradinas and Dr. Fernando Paradinas: pp. 60, 61 (bottom), 62,
    64 (both), 66, 67
Reverend W. B. Scott: p. 56

Avon County Library (Bristol Reference Library): p. 96
Borghese Gallery, Rome: p. 10
Reproduced by Courtesy of the Trustees of the British Museum: pp. 83, 86
    (top right)
Reproduced by Courtesy of the British Museum (Natural History): p. 117
The Trustees of Dove Cottage, Grasmere: p. 121 (both)
The Garrick Club, London: p. 48
The Goodsell Collection at Keats House, Hampstead: pp. 12, 13, 14 (three),
    15 (both), 16, 17 (both), 18 (bottom), 19 (both), 20, 21 (both)
The Houghton Library, Harvard, U.S.A: p. 120
The Greater London Council as Trustees of the Iveagh Bequest, Kenwood:
    p. 9 (both)
Reproduced by permission of the London Borough of Camden from the
    collection at Keats House, Hampstead: pp. 6 (both), 7, 11 (both), 18
    (top), 22 (three), 23, 24, 26 (three), 27, 28, 34, 39, 47, 49 (both), 50 (left),
    58 (left), 61 (top), 63, 65, 68 (both), 69, 72, 73 (bottom), 74, 75, 78 (left),
    79, 80, 81, 82, 89 (both), 98 (left), 100 (both), 103, 104 (left), 110, 111, 114
    (top), 119 (left)
Reproduced by permission of the Bursar and Fellows of Merton College,
    Oxford: p. 118
National Portrait Gallery, London: pp. 8 (right), 31, 33, 35 (bottom), 36, 40
    (bottom), 44 (left), 45, 50 (right), 52 (right), 53 (left), 55 (top), 56 (right),
    57, 59 (left), 76, 78 (right), 85, 86 (left and bottom), 90, 91, 93, 95, 97, 104
    (right), 106, 108, 109, 115, 119 (right)

123

INDEX